MW01230204

The G Code Glow-Up

A Marketing & Branding Workbook

Letrece R. Griffin

The G Code Glow-Up

Letrece R. Griffin

For booking inquiries, email
Letrece@LetreceG.com
www.LetreceG.com
@TheLetreceG on all social media

Dedication:

Take life one day at a time,

that's what a wise man said to me.

He said, "Life, in all its complexity

is the ultimate test for you and me."

When you walk, hold your head up high

for the master's watching you from the sky.

I know not what trouble lies ahead.

Before you fight, use your head.

It's time to leave the nest where you were born,

this journey you must make alone.

Spread your wings and fly.

There's a power deep inside you, an inner strength

you'll find in time of need -

The Glow!

"The Last Dragon"
Dwight David

Table of Contents

So, you are ready to start your business. You've finally made the decision to take the leap of faith and create a life on your own terms. You are diving head first into your passion and are now ready to embark upon the holy grail of entrepreneurship. You've got your DBA or LLC registered with the State. You've filed for your EIN with the IRS. You have paid for your logo and website to be built and now you are ready for the followers to start rolling in on your Instagram page.

But, you soon realize that all of the preparing, posting, and screaming from the top of your lungs is just the beginning of starting and growing a business. You never knew that the actual work BEGINS once you are ready to roll out your product or service to the world.

Today, we live in a world full of convenience. A world where we can access just about anything with a few swipes of an iPhone. We live in a world where you can check on everyone in your family, and completely catch up on their lives without actually talking to or seeing them. And while this world is convenient, it's also very scary. We are spending more time away from the things that we truly love in our lives in order to "keep up" with what's going on in our online world. Social media has become the new reality. We are living in a world in which people's actions are motivated more by what they want to post on their social media feed than the true authentic experiences they are having in their businesses and lives.

As a Digital Media Instructor on the high school level by day, and a businessman/creative by night, I have watched the trends of Marketing and Branding go from business cards, flyers, and posters to a complete social media online focus. We used to go inside of stores and talk to people about our businesses or network at conferences and meetups. Now, we just feel like Facebook and Instagram can solve all of our problems for us (and for free, might I add). We all want to look successful. We feel a tug at our egos when we see those brands online that seem to have it all together. Their colors, logo, IG story and feed all have the same cohesive vibe and wonder, "Why can't my business look and feel like that?" The answer is authenticity.

The brands that you love and crave are all true to themselves. They have figured out how to speak the language their customers understand; their needs. Your clients are only customers because they have a need and you are available to fulfill that need. When I was building my D.J./Photography company, Mr. Clean DJ, I noticed that there was a need for a D.J. company that focused on playing "family friendly" versions of your favorite songs. This was birthed out of an actual need that I had after creating a playlist for the D.J. that played at my wedding. I knew I didn't want my parents, Pastor, and church congregation listening to the dirty version of Juvenile's "Back That Thang Up." I quickly realized there was a need in the marketplace for that service to be offered.

This book is all about getting your brand together using a straightforward approach to growing a successful business. Letrece Griffin is not only a Branding and Marketing expert, she is already a celebrated, published author who teaches her clients and students to live their best lives through mindfulness, and self-love. This book is a deeper dive into the world of Online Marketing and Business. Her approach is straightforward, no-nonsense, and full of mental jewels that will spark the creative genius inside of you. If you are reading this right now, I can guarantee that you are in for a treat.

I've been knowing Letrece her entire life. "Why," you ask? Because she's my sister. Yes, my real sister (same mom, same dad). We grew up together watching our father run a successful trucking company. We have always been around business and were taught the basic principles of growing a successful business from the ground up. Letrece has been in Marketing and Artist Management for over 10 years with many successful artists and projects under her belt. We both graduated with top honors from Full Sail University with a Masters degree in Entertainment Business. Letrece has been honored for being an outstanding entrepreneur in her community and abroad.

Let this book help guide you in the right direction and grow your business. Really focus on the chapters that speak the most to you, and don't hesitate to revisit the parts that give you the most insight. Congratulations on making this investment into your future! You are now about to crack open "The G Code."

Ontario "O.T." Griffin
Founder, Mr. Clean DJ (@MrCleanDJ)
Creative Entrepreneur

I was born into a family that held a legacy all its own. From business owners to musicians and everything in between, my family has always carved their own lane. Perhaps it's truth in the name, Griffin. The word Griffin denotes strength, courage, and leadership. Growing up, I sometimes questioned how I could carve out a lane for myself in a sea of such vigor. I soon realized that by simply being myself and leaning into the legacy of my name, that I could make an impact. By taking the skills and knowledge that I had acquired, I became empowered to help others on their journey to greatness. But, none of this could happen if I was not real with myself. Leaning into my legacy was not about accepting handouts from family. But rather, upholding the character traits that a Griffin is known for. Being strong, being courageous, being a leader, being real... that is being a Griffin. That is being a G.

"Keeping it G," is my personal twist on "keeping it real." If you are like me, you found Dave Chappelle's "When Keeping it Real Goes Wrong" sketches hilarious! They are filled with scenarios where a person was too "real" and things went negative very quickly. For me, "keeping it G," is not about brutal honesty, but it is about unwavering integrity, excellence, and a willingness to stand up as a leader in uneasy times. This book is going to challenge you to "Keep it G" with yourself. You will need to make hard assessments and internal audits. It will even push you to take a good look at those around you. But, the end result will be a foundation that will hold solid despite the many hurdles that business and personal branding can bring.

The Glow-Up edition of this book is helping you build your empire, one brick at a time. With that in mind, I encourage you to complete the worksheets and "Glow-Up" activities in the order they are presented in the book. Doing so will help keep you organized as well as provide great reference points for you to look back on.

So, let's get ready to GLOW-UP!

Letrece R. Griffin

Learn

Know the Lingo

Have you ever been in a meeting and people start referencing a previous conversation that you weren't privy to? Suddenly, you're lost and not really sure of how to get up to speed. It's not a good feeling. The same is true when people are throwing around terms that you are unfamiliar with. In college, I picked up a little trick that I still do today. Whenever I was in a situation where someone said a word I did not know the meaning of, I simply wrote it down. When I had free time, I would look up the definition of the word and attempt to use it in a sentence later that day to reinforce the new term I learned. With the unending access to just about anything, thanks to smart phones, you can look up the definition of a word in real time while you are in the meeting and keep on pushing! But back then, I had to settle for waiting to research it later.

As a Mass Communications major, I was learning about the industry so quickly, but there were still elements that I did not know about until I began internships and attempting to get jobs. I'd take meetings and people would ask me things that I was honestly clueless about. Gratefully, I had wonderful people around who coached me through those tough spots and helped me gain the knowledge I needed to be successful.

One of the most important things I took away from those early experiences was the importance of knowing the lingo of the industry I was hoping to break into. This necessity is not to sound pompous or arrogant when speaking with clients or colleagues, but rather, to ensure that you are the sharpest in executing your tasks and are not wasting your time going down the wrong path simply due to ignorance.

Ok, so when it comes to Marketing and Branding, what's the lingo that you need to know? Well, let's start there ...

Marketing is promoting a product or service in hopes of selling to a consumer. Marketing can take multiple forms such as advertising or street team promotions. Now, this is not to be confused with **Publicity**, which is the attention that is garnered from Marketing tactics. Meaning, publicity is the act of other people and outlets talking about the product or service you have been marketing. For example, you design a t-shirt and advertise in a magazine about it being available for purchase. People begin buying your shirt and it becomes so popular that media outlets are beginning to do write-ups about the new shirt that everyone is loving. People are making posts on Instagram in your shirt and tagging you. You are getting media attention outside of the purchased advertising that you did to promote your product. Marketing are the messages you put out about yourself. Publicity are the messages others put out about you.

Publicity tactics are handled by **Publicists**, whose job it is to get other people to pay attention to your product or service and talk about it. When I say "talk about it," I am referring to writing news or blog articles, television interviews or spotlights, magazine articles, etc. Even though there is a fine line between Marketing and Publicity, have no doubt that both are needed for success. Think about it, if you are the only person talking about how wonderful your product is, not many will believe you. But, if you AND other people are vouching for how great your product works, then not only has your reach multiplied in the number of people who know about your product, but it gives you an extra layer of validity. Similar to someone being a reference for you in a job interview. You sold yourself during the interview, but the person's reference reinforced your initial assertions and sealed the deal.

So, as you and your business has grown in popularity, it is important to control the messaging and positive public perception that you hold. **Public Relations** is the art of doing so professionally. Public Relations is usually primarily thought of when there is a scandal and a spin is needed to clean it up. For example, an athlete with a family-friendly persona gets caught in a cheating scandal. I guarantee, that athlete employs a Public Relations firm or consultant to assist in changing his public perception from "cheater" back to "family man." While clean-up jobs are one aspect of PR, continued messaging of good will is advantageous for longevity. So, the fact that you are aware when companies make charitable offerings, that is PR at work. This is not to say that these companies are only doing these good deeds for how favorable it will make them look, but it is in fact a collateral byproduct.

Over time, these acts help build public perception and begins forming that company's brand. The word "brand" has probably become one of the most overused and misused words within the last few years. I'm sure you hear many people speaking about their brand, but may not be fully aware of what it really is. A **Brand** is a mixture of sentiments, principles, and actions that represent a person or company. In simpler terms, it is like a person's character. As you get to know someone overtime, you learn more about them and attach feelings to experiences you've shared. If you have grown to know that person as a truth-teller, but one day hear of them telling lies, you would not be quick to believe that because those actions are outside of the character you know that person to be. The same is true of a brand. As the consumer continues to patronize you and grows with your company, they too form expectations of you. So, if a company that is known for making juice for toddlers began also making alcohol, consumers would be confused that the new product does not align with the company's brand. The odds of the new alcohol venture being successful would be slim. **Branding** is the representation of these sentiments, principles, and actions that you are building. A visual representation of your brand is a logo. Your logo is not your brand, but rather the symbol that represents it. Your logo should be polished, professional, visually appealing and represent your overall brand well.

As your business grows, you may need assistance and begin looking for people to help you maintain your current workload and even help to solicit more business. Two roles that I often hear interchanged incorrectly is that of the manager and agent. A **Manager** is someone who handles your day-to-day operations and assists with the overall planning and execution of your business or career. This could include multiple tasks such as assisting with funds allocations, scheduling, contract negotiations, etc. Think of them similar to a project or office manager. Their compensation may be percentage based or they may receive a monthly fee or retainer.

An *Agent* is someone whose job is to represent you or your company in an effort to gain work, such as a booking or talent agent. Usually, they will get a percentage of the compensation received for the confirmed referrals made or jobs booked. If you're familiar with HBO's *Entourage*, Ari Gold was the quintessential agent. He was ruthless, bold, arrogant, and willing to do anything to close the deal for his client. In a cutthroat industry like entertainment, those types are indeed needed.

These key words we have reviewed are just the basics. Of course, there are plenty more where these came from. But, this is a good foundation to get you started.

Glow-Up Activity

Each person in your business plays a role. There is an important job for each person to play. At times, you may be wearing many hats and doing multiple jobs, but eventually, you'll need to relinquish tasks to those you trust and/or hire. Below, make a list of the roles you are currently playing, which ones can be assigned to someone else, and which ones you are currently in need of. A clear assessment of your current standing is a great benefit!

What roles are you currently playing?

Which tasks can be reassigned to someone else? List them below.

Which roles are you currently in need of? (For example, a manager).

G Code: "All the world's a stage, and all the men and women merely players; They have their exits and their entrances, and one man in his time plays many parts." – William Shakespeare

Get a Mentor

Learning is something that should never stop. Regardless of age, if you are open to it, you can truly learn something new every day. As children, we are so eager for knowledge and are sponges absorbing information all around us as we grow. However, for some, as we mature, we get settled in our ways and become complacent. We may not verbalize the mentality of "we know enough," but our actions reflect it. We have to vehemently reject this notion. To be most effective in Marketing and Branding, we must always be willing to learn. And, a part of that is acknowledging that we do not know everything and appreciating the value in learning from others. It is literally impossible for us to know it all, so relying on the knowledge and wisdom of others is a vital key to enhancing your success.

Finding a mentor is a crucial step in advancing your personal and business efforts. Now, admittedly, this may be easier said than done. To be quite honest, not everyone is willing to be forthcoming in sharing their knowledge and experiences. It may be out of fear that you will become competition, but I've always believed that sentiment is flawed. (We'll discuss later why I strongly believe that we are better together). Some are willing but just do not have the time to take on another mentee. Whatever the circumstance, don't get discouraged if it takes you a while to find the right match in an advisor.

A mentor's job is to be a well of resources. This may take various different shapes, but the end result is all about elevating you in areas that need improvement. And, just as it is impossible for you to know all things, it is unfair to think that one mentor can be all things to you. You may have multiple advisors that assist you in different aspects of your career. For example, you may have one that helps with resume building and interview skills while another may be in the industry you are building your career in and assists with introducing you to potential clients or advises on industry specific needs.

So, how do you go about finding a mentor? Start locally. Begin researching who are the key players in your area for the industry you are interested in. More than likely, if they are at the top of the industry, they will most likely have speaking engagements and/or reading materials where you can start. Attend the conferences and invest in reading the materials they have written on the subject matter. Only after doing so should you attempt contacting them. By doing so, you will have a great ice breaker to initiate a conversation. For example, your opening line could be, "I had the pleasure of hearing you speak at Loyola University in New Orleans a few months ago. I was very inspired by everything you shared. I am an aspiring writer and seeking guidance on how to get an internship with a magazine. I would be honored if you could share some tips that could assist me." Hopefully, your potential mentor will reply back thanking you for attending the speaking engagement and share some tips that can help you.

Another approach is more indirect but can be just as effective. Make yourself available and volunteer with whom you are seeking to gain knowledge from. Some of the best learning experiences you will have will be hands-on. If you are interested in event planning, you can offer to assist an event planner you admire. In a fast pace world, not many will turn down free help, especially if the volunteers show themselves to be reliable. Your eagerness to be selfless and help will prove to be beneficial in the experience and first-hand knowledge you gain by working alongside someone who is already working in the field you are attempting to succeed in.

Know the players of your industry. Be a student of the game. Being a good student sets you up for being a dynamic leader. You do not have to have direct contact with someone in order to learn from them. Social media has made everyone virtually accessible. There are numerous people that I follow online that I learn from daily. You can do the same. For example, if you are in journalism, Soledad O'Brien is an award-winning journalist who is a great person to follow online. Or, if the television industry is your thing, Mara Brock Akil is an amazing screenwriter who has given us shows like *Being Mary Jane, Girlfriends,* and *Love Is*. Her successes and struggles in the industry are definitely a good source to learn from. It was recently announced that her record-breaking series, *The Game*, will be returning with the original cast! That journey will undoubtedly be something interesting to follow as she resurrects this sitcom AGAIN.

So, get out there and get to it!

Glow-Up Activity

Make a list of the top 5 people who are potential mentors for you. What is a good contact for them (email, social media handle, etc.)?

1.

2.

3.

4.

5.

Why did you select these people?

What do you hope to gain from them?

G Code: Use these answers as driving forces to keep you focused on getting what you need from them. But remember, make yourself available to your potential mentor before asking for guidance.

Stay in Your Feelings

When you hear someone say that they were "in their feelings," it usually has a negative connotation. When making business decisions, it is often suggested that feelings or emotions should be removed from the situation in order to keep a logical view. However, when it comes to Marketing and Branding, staying in your feelings can actually be a good thing. "How," you may ask? Let me break it down.

"Emotional Branding" refers to the practice of building a campaign around feelings through the senses (sound, taste, touch, smell, and sight). Our human experiences attach memories with our senses. For instance, have you ever encountered a smell that reminded you of someone from your past? Or, heard a song that instantly put you in your feelings and reminded you of a person or place? These are all triggers that can be used to your benefit when marketing a product or service. Companies that use emotional branding overall have a deeper and more lasting relationship with clients.

The first step in achieving this goal is to do something that catches your audience's attention. This goes to how you introduce yourself (or your product) to the public. A great recent example of impactful emotional branding is the roll-out campaign of how Senator Kamala Harris introduced her candidacy for the 2020 Presidential election. She had us all in our feelings by officially announcing her candidacy on Martin Luther King Jr.'s holiday. Instead of trying to ignore her double minority, she completely leaned into them. Even the primary colors of her signs were giving a message. Using mainly yellow and purple, whose colors convey freshness, optimism, royalty and creativity, she was not only appealing to our sense of sight (who can miss a yellow sign?!) but also giving us underlining meanings as well. Unfortunately, to date, she has withdrawn from the 2020 presidential race. But, her campaign will be studied for years to come as she had one of the most impactful introductions to a presidential campaign.

Colors matter. Someone may see your street sign or logo before they even hear from you directly. So, real thought is needed when considering the colors that will represent you. Certain colors provoke certain emotions from consumers. It is important not to just select colors that you may like, but to make sure the colors are aligned with the message you want to send. For example, the color red has been proven to spark our appetites while the color blue is more calming and often associated with appetite suppressants. Take a look around, most major food chains have red as a primary color (McDonald's, Burger King, Dairy Queen, Red Lobster). And, many weight loss or healthy eating advertisements use the color blue.

When used properly, your feelings (and anticipating the emotions of your customer) will prove beneficial to your marketing success.

Glow-Up Activity

Business and Brand Storytelling is important. It tells your audience your "WHY." Use this space to begin formulating your "WHY."

- What do you do?

- Why do you do it? (your backstory)

- Who are you talking to in explaining your "WHY?"

- WHY should your audience care?

- What conflict or problem does your "WHY" answer or solve?

G Code: "He who has a why to live for can bear almost any how." - Friedrich Nietzsche

Glow-Up Activity

Research and select brand colors that coincide with your business. Here are some prompts to help you get in and stay in your feelings.

- What do you hope your customer feels when thinking about your product or service (for example – relaxed, excited, hungry, motivated) and why?

- Building on that feeling, what action do you hope your potential customer will take?

- Create a tagline for your business or personal brand that is catchy and will draw people to learn more about you and your company.

Know Your Target Market

Ok, so you have figured out what your message is (and what visuals you will use to help spread that message). Now, you need to spread the word. But, who exactly are you spreading that message to? Who is your target audience? And, how can you ensure that you reach them? The answer is found in research and proper execution.

Your target market is the audience that your product or service should be aimed towards. If you do not take the time to analyze your target market, you will waste a lot of time and money with little results. I'll give you a real-life example that I experienced. I once worked with a concert promoter who threw predominately blues and soul concerts. As his company attempted to expand to do shows in different cities, he found that ticket sales were not as high as projected. I was hired to assist with the Marketing and Promotions of the concerts. Upon researching what advertising channels were being utilized, I discovered that the company was not advertising with the correct radio station for the area. The company had radio spots on popular stations, but they did not really play the type of music that the concerts were geared towards. Once we began running advertisements on the stations that played mostly soul and blues music, ticket sales began to increase significantly. The promoter was just thinking "urban radio" and didn't factor in how that market is segmented. It wasn't a matter of how much money was being spent, but that the marketing dollars were being spent correctly.

There are four main things to consider when researching your target market: demographics, geography, spending habits, and how your product or service fulfills a need or want for the consumer. Let's do a quick rundown.

First, demographics is your audience's population (age, race, gender, etc.). Second, geography is your audience's location. Depending on how large of a campaign you are constructing, it can be regional or hyper-segmented by variables such as zip code. Next, spending habits in this context is more related to analyzing what ways your consumers spend their money (not so much as to what they are spending their money on). For example, is your audience more likely to make online purchases? Or, does your audience show signs of making purchases from Instagram sponsored advertisements? Finally, you want to show the consumer that your product or service is beneficial to them. Steve Jobs, co-founder of Apple, is noted for saying, "People don't know what they want until you show it to them." You may have an amazing idea that no one even realizes they need yet! Don't let that stop you. It is your task to find the correct channels to get your message out to *your* audience that will patronize you.

Now you are getting to the part where it is crucial that you work smarter, not harder. By doing these research steps beforehand, you are equipping yourself for the greatest chance of success. After you've done this preliminary research, it should give you an answer regarding which channels should be used to reach your desired audience. Channels are the avenues used to deliver your Marketing messages (for example: television, radio, magazines, social media, etc.). By working smarter, you will not just spend money on every channel available, rather, you will select the ones that your research shows will connect with your audience. If your target audience is millennials, then social media is a safe route to advertise. On the other hand, although persons over 60 years old can also be tech-savvy, it is more likely that traditional media outlets such as television or radio would be most successful in reaching them.

Remember, just like a bullseye target, almost hitting the mark doesn't count. Let your research guide you on where your audience is and how to reach them. Don't miss your mark!

Glow-Up Activity

Utilize this space to document your target market.

DEMOGRAPHICS	GEOGRAPHY	SPENDING HABITS	HOW IT FULFILLS WANTS/NEEDS

Glow-Up Activity

Being flexible is essential to success. This activity will allow you to practice adjusting your message for your target audience and correct channel.

Write a marketing message below (for example: soliciting people to purchase your new line of candles). Tailor that message to fit your target market using the research you gathered above.

Alter the message above to be a Facebook post. Write it below.

Create that message to fit on Twitter (being mindful of the 280-character count limit to date). Write it below.

Change that message to work for Instagram (being mindful that platform works best with photos, gifs, videos, etc.)

Create that post for LinkedIn. Write it below.

Plan

Get an Elevator Speech

Imagine you find yourself on an elevator with Oprah Winfrey. After you shake back from the initial shock, and telling her how amazing she is, you find the nerve to tell her you have a business. She simply responds, "Nice. Tell me about it." Your elevator ride is only about a minute, which is how long you have to be effective and memorable. Hence, the "elevator speech," a short 2-3 sentence explanation of you, your product, or service. Of course, you cannot tell everything about your business in only a couple of sentences, but you can say enough to give an overall explanation and to entice the person you are speaking to in wanting to get more information.

Now, let's be real. The odds that you will actually be on an elevator with Oprah is really slim, but the chances that you may run into a viable connection at a networking event is very possible. The same theory applies. You need to explain your product or service in a short amount of time. People have short attention spans. Even if they are truly interested in learning about what you have to offer, they do not want to listen to you ramble as you struggle to explain your product. Think of it this way, how can you expect anyone to know what you are about if you yourself are unable to articulate it?

I know, your dreams are big! Your potential is huge! Your product will change the game! How can you possibly sum all of that into a one-minute spill? It is okay if you need to work your way down. Start with writing a mission statement. Your mission statement should define your purpose and clearly state who (or what) you are. It should be specific in explaining why your company exists (what need does it meet). Finally, it should inspire. Almost like a motto or creed, it should motivate you and your employees as to why they work for or follow the mission of the company.

Once you've completed your full mission statement, you can use that to condense it down to your elevator speech. Be sure that your speech explains these key points: explains what you do, identifies a tangible goal, highlights you (or your products), and satisfies a need. To end your speech, you should engage the person you are speaking to with a question that prompts conversation. And of course, you should have a business card to give. Now, arguments have been made that in today's high-tech world, virtual or e-cards are the next wave. While that may be true, most people still want something in their hands they can take away.

You should practice your elevator speech so that it becomes fluid and second nature to you. When delivering it, it should not sound rehearsed. This is your business, no one knows it better than you. You have put in a lot of time and work into this. So, when you speak about it, you should be passionate and energetic. The person you are speaking to should feel excited about the opportunity you have shared with them.

Another great thing about having a good elevator speech is that it can be used as your litmus test when making business decisions. It can also help to keep your business on track. You should refer back to it and ask, "Will taking this action support my mission?" If it does, then it is worth exploring. If it does not then perhaps it is not the right opportunity for you. Remember that your elevator speech is an ever-evolving piece of work. While the core of what you are saying will remain the same, your delivery or certain points may be emphasized depending on your audience. For instance, if you are speaking to a potential investor, your speech may lean more on how your business can generate a great return on investment. But, if you are speaking to someone who is a graphic designer, you may stress how your company could be a great platform to showcase their designs.

Your words matter. And, choosing your words concisely is a powerful tool in your Marketing and Branding skillset.

Glow-Up Activity

Utilize this space to begin curating your elevator speech. Remember, you do not have to be in an actual elevator to share your story. Practice this networking tactic whenever possible.

- Write your mission statement (this should not only include what you do or represent, but why).

- What is the condensed version of your above statement? Write it below. Remember, it should be stated in less than 2 minutes.

G Code: "A mission statement is not something you write overnight... But fundamentally, your mission statement becomes your constitution, the solid expression of your vision and values. It becomes the criterion by which you measure everything else in your life." – Stephen Covey

Do your SWOTs

Nope, this is not a misprint. I'm not telling you to do squats (but, there is nothing wrong with doing those too). A major part of your planning process should be to do a SWOT Analysis. Knowledge is indeed power, and a thorough SWOT Analysis is the linchpin to effective Marketing.

SWOT stands for Strengths, Weaknesses, Opportunities, and Threats. These four categories will make or break your Marketing and Branding efforts. It is the framework of the strategic plan needed for a successful brand campaign. It analyzes how sustainable your product or service will be for the market you are trying to operate in. I know all of this can sound really heavy, but actually writing out your SWOT does not have to be cumbersome. I advise doing this exercise with a group of people you trust, reference back to those advisors or mentors we spoke about earlier. They can be a great resource in assisting with this.

Many map out their SWOT in a four-box format by drawing a large box and separating it into a grid with four spaces, then placing a title in each. You then list items within each box that match its title. But honestly, you can list your SWOT however is most comfortable for you and allows you to process the information best.

First are your company's strengths. This list should be compiled of all the things you do well. What are your greatest assets? What makes your company unique? It is ok to brag and list all that you excel in, however, be realistic. If you know your bakery doesn't really have the best strawberry cupcakes in the city, do not list that as a strength. Second, is the list of your company's weaknesses. This may be painful to admit, but we all have things that we can improve on. Take a sobering look in the mirror and see where you (or your product/service) needs development. This list can range from logistical process operations to if your website is user-friendly. Third, is the list of what opportunities are available. What new openings or leads for business is available? Are there opportunities for you or your business to grow and expand? Finally, is the list of your threats. Basically, who (or what) is your competition? Also noteworthy in this section are other factors that may threaten the success of your business. This could include the economy, social trends, or political climate.

Once you have completed your SWOT Analysis, then you can formulate a plan that addresses what you have discovered. Draw from the knowledge you have gained and continue to build on your strengths, work to improve and correct your weaknesses, take advantage of the opportunities, and do your best to eliminate the threats. During this time, you can also take a deeper dive into separating your needs versus your wants. As you work to build your brand, I'm sure you will have big ideas. It is important to not have that cloud your judgement to what is necessary now. In no way am I suggesting that you dim your light or sell yourself short in what your dreams are. I am merely cautioning you to not over-extend yourself, especially as you are in the beginning stages. For example, do you really *need* a launch party with a budget that exceeds $12,000, or is that just something you *want*? More than likely, you can throw a launch party that can be just as effective and community driven for a much smaller price tag.

Arming yourself with the knowledge you have gained from your SWOT Analysis, coupled with your ambition and grit, you are well on your way to forming a brand that will stand the test of time.

Glow-Up Activity

Be sure to "Keep it G" with yourself on this activity when you do your SWOTs.

STRENGTHS	WEAKNESSES
OPPORTUNITIES	THREATS

What action steps can you take to address each item?

Set Goals

In Marketing, you want to do the most you can to set yourself up for success. A major key in doing so is to set goals. During consultations, one of the first questions I always ask is, "What is your goal?" This may seem like a no-brainer type question, but if you approach this question with serious thought and organization, it will prove itself to be beneficial in achieving longevity and success. Having your goals outlined provides a roadmap to where you hope to go. Use it as your navigational system. Think of it as a road trip. On a road trip, you will have pit stops, unforeseen traffic jams, or even car trouble. But, you know where you are headed so you keep on the path.

When setting goals, they should include three main landmarks. Your goals should be specific, realistic, and measurable. It is not enough to say that you want your clothing line to be in stores. You need to start by being specific about what stores or online platforms you'd like for your merchandise to be sold. When setting goals, drill down with specificity. Adding a measurable element also keeps you accountable and helps to provide a benchmark if you are on track to achieving your goal. For example, by adding a quantity and/or specific deadline, you are giving yourself something tangible to work toward. But, I must caution you in doing this to also be realistic. It is not helpful to give yourself an unattainable goal. While anything is possible, you have to factor in if it is actually plausible. Is it possible that you could win the lottery and use those winnings to fund your business? Sure, anything is *possible*. But, what are the odds that could actually happen? Researchers give that chance about 1 in 300 million. So, it would be better for you to have a more realistic goal on how to fund your business.

Using our "clothing line" example from earlier, a goal that is specific, realistic, and measurable would be, "I want my 'LOVE' t-shirt line to be sold in the southern region of Macy's stores by the Spring of 2020." With this statement, you have clearly stated exactly what outlet you want which t-shirt line to be sold and have also attached a timeline to it.

Another important tip about setting realistic goals starts to take place once you've gained customers and are dealing with clients. Successful Marketing and Brand loyalty are directly tied to the timeline goals you set for your customers. I've seen talented graphic designers whose business didn't grow due to customer's complaints that they did not receive their designs in the timeline promised. If you know you cannot complete a project in two days, do not tell your customer that you can. It is better to under promise and over deliver. You should tell your client that the turnaround time for their project to be completed is five business days, then, when you complete it in three, they are overly pleased.

Above all, an important thing about setting goals is that they need to be written down (or typed, or drawn … whatever platform you use to muse). The point is, it does not just need to live in your head. Once you take the time to release your goals into the atmosphere, then they are no longer just dreams or aspirations. They are something real that you are working toward. Not everyone wants to go all out with creating vision boards, and that is okay. If creating those boards help you to map out your goals, then by all means, do it. But, maybe all you need is a piece of paper in a notebook next to your bed where you write down blurbs as they come to you. Or, perhaps you have sticky notes all over your desk or home with your goals, aspirations, or plans. If I can paraphrase Erykah Badu here, "Write it down and watch it get real."

Glow-Up Activity

Set five goals for your business and/or personal brand that are specific, realistic, and measurable.

1.

2.

3.

4.

5.

G Code: Verify how your goals are "measurable" by checking your analytics. Check on your goal's progress monthly, quarterly, etc. Identify what works for you. Build on what is working and adjust what is not.

Be Authentic

DO. NOT. FAKE. IT. TILL. YOU. MAKE. IT.

I know we have all heard that term before. In life, it is a good motivational theme to live by. Sometimes, you do have to present yourself and operate as if you are already there. But, in Marketing and Branding, "faking it" will quickly kill your efforts and scar your digital imprint.

A successful brand is built on authenticity. Regardless of the industry, people and customers gravitate towards what they perceive as real. You and your brand should be based on your true beliefs, characteristics, and goals. Think about the videos that go viral or the social media comedians that have the most success. They all are operating from a place of truth. I participated in a panel discussion regarding diversity in filmmaking recently. As the Executive Producer of a documentary on colorism, I was invited to share my thoughts on the representation of minorities in entertainment and film. The discussion was very enlightening and challenging all at once. One of the biggest takeaways everyone in the room seemed to agree with was that some of the most successful films (and even those that stand the test of time as being classic) are those that have an authentic voice and representation. They are films that speak their truth. Recent examples of these films include *Black Panther* and *Moonlight*.

Being authentic is about being true. Everyone may not like your truth. You have to be prepared to face that. But, just as there will be people who may not agree with you, there will be those who genuinely support you. That is your audience. Those are the people you should focus on.

I had the pleasure of leading a promotional team in the southern region for Grammy award-winning artist, PJ Morton. He dropped a jewel of wisdom that I have always carried with me. He explained how he had to get out of the mindset of trying to make music for everyone and stay true to making the music that represented him and what was in his heart. When he did that, thanks to the internet and social media, his audience found him. And, that is remarkable when you think about it. By just continuing to do what you love from a place of being genuine, your supporters will find you. How many videos have your shared with friends because you found them funny, entertaining, or illuminating? That is authentic "word of mouth" Marketing.

With this as a premise, please, do not purchase followers for your social media platforms. I'll say it again for the people in the back. Do not purchase followers for your social media platforms. I know you want to look like you are already popping with thousands of followers, but because those followers are fake, you are not getting real engagement with an audience, which is what you want. It is better to have a lower follower count with high engagement than to have it the other way around. Engagement is how people respond to your posts (are they liking, commenting, and/or sharing your content).

Imagine you had 1,500 followers on Instagram. You make a post telling people to come out for an event you are hosting. Because these are actual followers, your message is landing with real people who will likely respond and share your content. Research suggests that on average, 4% of your follower count actually engages with your content. Now, imagine you have 15,000 bought followers on Instagram. You release the same post. Research shows that the engagement ratio for fake followers is only 1%. So, while your follower count is higher, your engagement ratio is lower. So, at face value, you may look like you're doing well, but in reality, you are not.

Another important key to remember about Marketing is that your online audience needs to be treated with respect. It can often get lost when you spend so much time behind a smart phone or computer, but these are real people you are communicating with. Don't just data dumb information on your audience and never engage them in conversation. They deserve to be listened to, responded to, and shown appreciation.

These are your consumers. They are your audience, so take care of your people. Now, that is being real.

Build

Create Calls to Action

I used to hate the term "Bossy." Probably because I am female, it was often thrown at me with a negative connotation. But, as I grew older, I no longer cared how people perceived my demeanor. I often found myself in leadership positions because I was unafraid to say what others were too shy to say aloud. So, for me, the word "Bossy" was just a different way of saying that I was willing to speak my mind, even if that meant telling others what needed to be done.

In Marketing, this characteristic is a must. Effective Marketing is about persuading your audience to think a certain way, buy a certain product, or take a particular action. That is pretty much a fancy way of saying that Marketing is telling people what to do. The technical term for this is creating "Calls to Action," or CTA. It may seem like common sense, but you need to instruct your audience on what you would like for them to do. There are a few tricks to make sure they follow your lead.

First, use command verbs such as "click," "visit," "follow," or "buy." I know it sounds simple and you may even think that it should go without saying, but never assume. Be plain in telling your audience exactly what you want them to do. "Click the link in my bio," "Follow my friend @TheLetreceG for details," or "Buy my new CD now." Giving explicit directions does not leave room for misunderstanding. There isn't a lot of room for ambiguity in Marketing.

Next, after telling your audience what to do, they need to be routed to a location so they can complete that action. For example, if you post on Facebook telling people to donate to your fundraiser, a link should be provided that leads them to where they can make that donation. People are impulse buyers. I am ashamed to admit that Instagram ads have gotten me quite a few times. Make it simple for consumers to see your CTA, and then easily find where they can follow what you are looking for them to do.

Finally, really highly charged CTA's touch on audience's emotions (recall back to why staying in your feelings is good Marketing). By using stories or words that provoke certain emotions, you can persuade your audience to take the action you desire. Advertisers have been doing this for years. We all remember those animal cruelty commercials with that sad song, "In the arms of an angel." Throughout the commercial, you were constantly being prompted to act by calling the number on the screen. At the end, we wanted to save all of those poor animals.

Calls to Action are often considered one of the most important elements of a Marketing campaign. You've gotten your potential client interested, but you haven't given them instructions or a clear route on how to find you or your product. That is an opportunity lost. In my days of artist management, I cannot tell you how many demo CDs I received that had no contact information on them. Instances where I was interested in working with the artist, I had no way of reaching them. Regardless if your product is baked goods, clothing, or music, every product should have calls to action on them, even if that is just instructions on how you can be reached (website, email address, phone number, or social media).

Glow-Up Activity

Create a content calendar for one week. Be sure to include "Calls to Action" (CTA) and create content that is both compelling and informative for your audience.

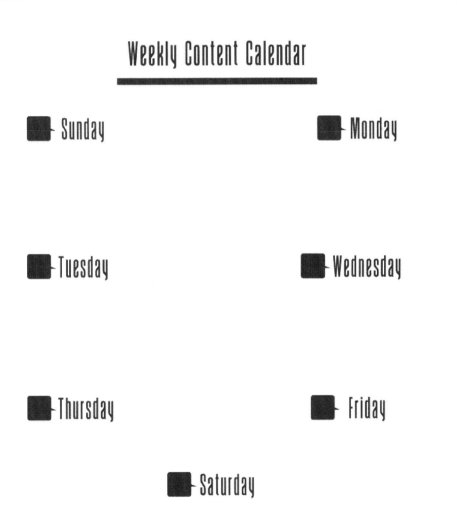

Weekly Content Calendar

◼ Sunday

◼ Monday

◼ Tuesday

◼ Wednesday

◼ Thursday

◼ Friday

◼ Saturday

Glow-Up Activity

Take one post from the above activity. Below, you will pitch this content idea three different ways. Essentially, come up with three unique (different) ways to get someone to click the link in your bio (or the link provided in the post). Remember, to utilize various tactics such as humor and/or relatability to keep your audience engaged and willing to adhere to your call to action prompts.

- Post One:

- Post Two:

- Post Three:

G Code: "Be content to act, and leave the talking to others." - Baltasar Gracian

Make Connections

If the past few years have taught me anything, it is that we are truly better together! Regardless of the size of the city you live, there is enough room for everyone to shine and be successful. In actuality, the chances are probably increased if you partner with people who have common goals. We have to reject the stereotype of crabs in a barrel trying to bring each other down. We can be and are better than that.

Understandably, making connections and networking is not so easy for everyone. You may have the desire to do so, but actually sparking a conversation with a stranger can seem intimidating. As with anything, start with research. Find out what events are happening in your area related to your industry of interest. For instance, are there any art exhibits, financial conferences, or community meetings taking place? Attend these events in the hopes of meeting likeminded people you can connect with. Or, there may be actual networking events that will mesh together people from various industries. Those are great to attend as well.

While at these events, this is where your elevator speech comes in. But, don't just walk up to people and start telling them about yourself. It is always better to ask the person you are speaking to about themselves first. After engaging in conversation, hopefully you have found an area of mutual interest and an opportunity to share about yourself has arisen. Of course, be sure to exchange contact information (even if it is just following each other on social media). You'll need some kind of way to keep in touch. Also, as a courtesy, be sure not to take up too much of that person's time.

Next is a step that many people neglect when networking, which is the follow-up. Within 24-48 hours of meeting someone, you should follow up via that person's preferred method of contact, which hopefully you discovered during the conversation you had with them. If you are unsure, an email is a safe bet. During this communication, you should express how pleased you were with meeting them. Mention elements of your conversation and suggest a call or meeting where the two of you can continue to build on your initial conversation.

A good rule of thumb is to offer before you ask. Meaning, before you ask for a favor, you should offer your services first. Or, present an opportunity where it is clear that both parties would benefit. Also, do not be afraid to share resources. Just as you hope that the people you meet will be forthcoming with you, that sentiment should be reciprocated. Building genuine connections is not about competition, but about building together.

Now, to be real, it is true that you cannot necessarily work with everyone. But, on the same token, you should not be afraid to collaborate with others. If you are like me, you may have been burned a time or two by people you thought had good intentions. I know the pain and frustration of that can make you rigid. However, do not allow that to prevent you from connecting with the slew of amazing people that are around you and are also looking for ways to enhance their communities and industries. The connections I have made over the last few years have enhanced my life in ways I could not have imagined. I have formed lasting friendships and bonds with people because I stepped out of my comfort zone and adapted the mentality that we are better together.

Glow-Up Activity

Thinking of ways to make connections in your city, use the space below to make a list of networking events you can attend and/or people who you wish to connect with.

List 5 events in your city that would be good for networking:

1.

2.

3.

4.

5.

List 5 people who you would like to connect with. What are good contact details for each person.

1.

2.

3.

4.

5.

G Code: "Your network is your net worth." – Porter Gale

Make your Presence a Present

I have had the infamous "chicken and egg" debate with colleagues on several occasions. Many squabble over what came first, the chicken or the egg. I always like to pose the question, "In business, what comes first, power or respect?" Both are attributes that many aspire to. But, what is more important? Which is more sustainable in maintaining relationships and longevity for your brand? If you ask me, I would say respect. Respect is something that can only be earned. I know people who have power that are not respected. But, you cannot really respect someone without revering them with an essence of power. A truly powerful person or brand must be respected first.

By operating with integrity and excellence, you begin building respect for yourself and your brand. This process is slow. It does not happen overnight. It is about making the best choice at every turn, and going above and beyond for your customer base whenever possible. Doing this consistently builds your reputation. A strong reputation for excellence cannot help but be respected. And, as that continues to build, the power that comes along with it is a currency more valuable than money. You are building social currency, which is the existing and potential resources that come along with the presence of you and your brand. Yes, you read that correctly. Just your presence holds a currency. If you have a reputation of excellence, your presence carries an undeniable currency. I'm sure you may have attended an event before where people were just excited that you were even there. That is because they realize the value of your presence and are appreciative that you took the time to attend their event.

Your social currency is your co-sign. Just as you should be cautious on who you would co-sign or vouch for, you should be just as protective of your social currency. When you agree to partner with someone or co-sponsor an event, you are leveraging your social currency. You are telling your audience that you believe in this effort. That should not be taken lightly. Even when you are seen attending an event or organizational meeting, you are also spending your social currency. You are spending social currency on whatever you are investing your time into. Just as you would not throw money away haphazardly, you should not spend your social currency carelessly.

Now, please do not take this the wrong way. I am not saying you should not be sociable and support others. As I stated in the previous chapter, we are better together. I am, however, advising that you be cautious on how you spend your time and with whom. Your reputation and time are much too valuable to waste it. Instead of just going out to be seen, prioritize your time accurately. Take the time to build your skillset by getting additional credentials, take webinar courses that will benefit your business, or attend community engagement sessions that will better the lives of those around you. Be purposeful with your time and intentions. Realize that merely your presence brings value.

So, with all of this in mind, how do you make your presence a present? By spending your social currency wisely. An additional way to bank your social currency is in your digital imprint and the content you produce. There is nothing wrong with posting funny memes, we've all done it, but if that is all your online presence shows, then you are not capitalizing on all that your social currency could be. Your social currency can sky rocket if you are releasing content that others find valuable and are sharing. Keep in mind that the content you release is not just online. It can be comprised of your goods and services, events, and/or speaking engagements. Of course, your online content can be vast as well. It could be blog posts, podcasts, webinars, digital music releases, or online galleries.

Your presence, whether online or in person, is another form of your wealth. Respect it. Use it wisely. And, leverage it to benefit your brand, your circle of influence, and those you are in partnership with.

Glow-Up Activity

Below, you will have some practice transforming your social currency into compelling content.

List an example of a product or service that you offer below. If you're working on your personal brand, list something about yourself that you want to be known for (or that your audience perceives you as).

Translate that item (or attribute) into an interesting piece of content. It can be a blog post, social media caption, press release, etc. Be sure to not just show your product/service, but also address what makes it different and why people should care. Does it address a need?

G Code: "Influence is NOT popularity." – Brian Solis

Be Bold. Be Dope.

One of my favorite comedians is the legend, Chris Rock. He has this bit about what men should do to convince women to do what they want. He jokingly explains that women respond to boldness and strength, so anything that is asked with a timid approach won't get done. The same is true for Marketing. You have to be bold to get results. The essence of being bold is about knowing who you are and standing firm in that. Projecting that strength into your work and how you present yourself is a valuable asset to your overall brand.

Despite knowing this, I have to admit, being bold is not always an easy task. There are times when I doubt myself, I wonder if I am making the right decisions, and as hard as I may be working, there is always the thought in the back of my head that I could be going harder. There are times when I don't want to stand out from the crowd, when I just want to be me. Then, I realize that "just being me" *is* what makes me stand out from the crowd. The same is true for you. Having the ability to flip doubtful sentiments will help you fuel your boldness. Do not shy away from the things that set you apart, rather, lean into them.

The way that you view yourself effects every aspect of your life and business. You set the standard for how you build your brand and how the consumer will respond to it. It is important that you know your worth and don't second guess it. Doing so will give you a firm foundation on how you shape your Marketing campaigns and business. It is perfectly okay to demand what you deserve. Demands are easily catered to when a person has put in the work and has a track record of success that can be referenced.

As an event and concert producer, I often receive riders from artists that list all of their personal demands. Some are modest requests like bottled water, sodas and food. Others are more extravagant and specific, like listing certain brands of liquor, food preparation demands, and room décor. Usually, the more accomplished the artist, the greater the demands. What I've found, is that if the artist has a strong reputation for success, then the promoters and venue have no problem with meeting those demands. However, if the artist is relatively new or has not had a string of successful shows, then people are unwilling to invest more into rider demands. Point being, you have to put in the work first in order to make demands. Your work ethic and product have to be able to back up your requests. If the consumer finds substance in what you're offering, they will not mind paying a fair price.

Your boldness coupled with being dope is a fierce combination. Being dope is all about your unique spin on the world. You have a distinctive spark that allows you to see things differently. Use that to your advantage. I lead a think-tank session with a group of teenagers once that was very eye-opening to this theory. I gave them a simple instruction, "You are tasked with coming up with a way to sell ice cream," I advised. That group of young people came up with about 17 different ideas on how to sell ice cream. Some created jingles, others created special discounts and promotional offerings, while others used a more basic approach in emphasizing how ice cream is such a beloved dessert. It blew me away that so many different approaches were drawn out of the same simple instruction. It showed that we all see things differently, and that is amazing. There was not just one right answer, just as there is not just one path to success.

Being bold and being dope is about being yourself, but being the absolute best version of that. In order to do so, you've got to put the work in. Nothing worth anything comes easy. Do not expect anything from others that you are not willing to do yourself. If you expect clients to patronize you, you have to provide a service worth paying for. Eliminate the "good enough" attitude from your mentality. If you are working on something and find yourself saying "that's good enough," stop it! Go back and keep working on it until you are fully satisfied with the outcome. Continue to seek knowledge, not just for your own edification, but to equip you with providing better service to your consumer base, along with elevating and effecting change in your industry.

Nothing is bolder and more dope than leaving a positive and lasting mark on society.

Execute

Face your Fears

Since I was a little girl, I've always liked horror movies. Usually when you speak to people who like horror films, they'll tell you that they don't find them scary. I, however, really felt scared while watching these movies. But, oddly enough, I liked the thrill of the feeling of being scared. My all-time favorite horror villain is Freddy Kreuger. His badly burned skin, knives for fingers, and sadistic humor haunted me. The fact that you weren't even safe in your sleep really put him on a whole other level. The film franchise had a successful run, and with each new movie, I was at the theatre, excited about being scared. But, each night, I'd have a nightmare that Freddy was trying to kill me and it would leave me restless and terrified. The anxiety I felt running for my life in those nightmares felt so real.

During one of these dreams, I remember running down a dark street with Freddy not far behind. He was taunting me and reveling in the fact that he would soon catch and kill me. In a spark of genius, I just stopped running. I realized that half the fun for Freddy was in the chase. So, if I did not give him that power and just turn and face my fear, then I would be okay. My logical brain was telling my dream-state brain, "What's the worst that can happen? If he kills you, it doesn't matter. This isn't real. It's only a dream." So, I stopped running. I turned around and said, "Ok man, just go ahead and kill me and get it over with." The look of confusion on Freddy's face was priceless! When I faced him, he no longer had an interest in terrorizing me. He left me alone, and I woke up, safe and sound in my bed and at peace. As I've gotten older and experienced life, I realized that this is a metaphor for taking chances in business. The feelings of being scared and fearful were real, but the actuality of them were not. It was only a dream. Even though it may have felt like it, Freddy was not a real person trying to kill me. Then, I realized that once I had the courage to step up and face my fear, I was able to overcome it.

You also have the power to face and overcome the feelings of fear that may be haunting you. Interscope Records and Beats Electronics co-founder, Jimmy

Iovine, gave an interesting take on fear that I have carried with me. "If you can figure out a way to wrestle that fear to push you from behind rather than it to stand in front of you, that's very powerful," he stated. He is acknowledging that feelings of fear are real, but that you can also use them as catalysts instead of allowing them to be roadblocks. Just as I was excited about being scared in the theatre when seeing Freddy Krueger, you can use that scared energy to motivate you instead of paralyze you. Allow fear to be the wind at your back that pushes you to greatness, not the windstorm that prevents you from succeeding.

Fear has levels to it. Fear of failure is something that many people grapple with. It can be scary to share your ideas with the world, particularly for those who operate in creative spaces. You may have doubts if people will understand or appreciate your work. Truth be told, we all have been there. It is important to remember that Marketing, especially in its beginning stages of implementation, involves a lot of trial and error. As you work to learn your audience's needs and trends, you will experiment on ways to effectively reach them and capitalize on your efforts. Some things will work, others will not. And, that is okay. Failure is a part of the process to success that can sometimes seem slow. But, slow motion is better than no motion. Even small steps count toward your success.

Actor and icon Will Smith started an Instagram account a little over two years ago and it has been the best thing to happen to social media in a long time. His account is a great source for not only creative inspiration, but motivation in general as we all work to be better and produce better products. In one of his posts, he elaborated on the concept of failure. He advised that we should "fail early, fail often, and fail forward." He explained that if we accept and embrace failure as a part of the process that gets us closer to achieving success, then we would not shun or belittle it. Rather, we would embrace it for getting us closer to what we are working towards. He explains that we grow the most when we learn from our failures. "Failure actually helps you recognize the areas where you need to evolve," Smith stated. If used as a learning tool, failure is a valuable commodity in your Marketing and Branding toolkit.

Glow-Up Activity

Think over your career and list what you would consider to be your top three failures.

1.

2.

3.

Considering what you listed above, what did you learn and/or gain from these "failures?"

Are there missteps that you can adjust to enhance your career moving forward

Move in Silence

Now, I know what you're probably thinking. The concept of moving in silence seems to be a direct contradiction to the core definition of what Marketing is. After all, Marketing is about promoting and announcing what you have going on. But, hear me out.

The first time I heard the phrase, "Loose lips sink ships," was on Tupac Shakur's 1993 single "I Get Around." I've never forgotten that line. The proverbial light bulb went off in my head. It was like Tupac was giving me a life lesson, being that if you talk too much then it'll be to your detriment. Thinking back on it, I started to implement this as one of my cardinal rules. I became very selective on who I shared plans with and even more selective on who I accepted counsel from. In doing so, I learned the importance of knowing when to speak and the importance of my words. As I blossomed into my career, this concept proved to be even more true.

A critical component of Marketing is about timing. Several factors must be considered when thinking how the effect of timing relates to your Marketing efforts. Social climate is a major one. This takes into account how society as a whole perceives certain issues relevant to present day. A good example of this theory is online dating. Presently, the acceptance of online dating as a viable option is much more widespread than it was just a few years ago. So, if you created a dating app and attempted to market it, you would have more success now than you would have if you attempted to do so 10 years ago. The timing affected the chances of success.

Another example of timing having an effect on your Marketing efforts is your ability to exude patience. I know the feeling of being so excited about what you're working on that you cannot wait to share it with the public. It's like an itch that you just have to scratch. But, sharing details with the public too soon can work against you. I've seen many Marketing campaigns fail due to people releasing information prematurely. Often times, it is just that proper contingencies are not in place for when your audience does receive your Marketing message. For example, we spoke in an earlier chapter about calls to action; you may be so eager to put out your call to action (or announcement) but do not have anything for the consumer to actually do. That is a wasted Marketing opportunity. Let me give you a tangible example of this.

I once saw a Facebook post from an artist stating that his single would be released soon and to visit his website. At face value, there may not seem to be anything wrong with this. But, as we take a closer look, you will see the missed opportunities due to impatience. The artist's website was just a landing page, so it did not give any additional information about the upcoming release. It would have been helpful to at least been able to say a season of the year that consumers could expect his music (i.e. Summer 2020). Also, he did not have any mechanism in place to capture information from those he routed to his website. An email sign-up list on his landing page would have been a perfect way to stay in touch with his audience, keep them engaged, and to actually give them something to do when visiting his site. Building up an email database is a very important means of communicating in Marketing. You have to be prepared for your audience. In this example, the artist should have been patient and continued to work and move in silence on his music until he had a seasonal date of his release and a way to capture contact information from his followers.

Another noteworthy concept of moving in silence is allowing your actions to speak louder than your words. People are generally skeptical of words at face value. They put more stock into what they see and know to be true. You build a trust with your customer by what you do for them, not just by the words you say (or post). If you provide a quality product and excellent customer service, those are actions that your client base can build trust in. Your actions can be your best (and worst) publicist. Consistent actions that reflect integrity is a strong commodity to have as you build your Marketing and Branding efforts. Do not announce your moves before they are made. Trust me, people will see them once they're done. Nothing is worse than putting out Marketing messages that you do not follow through with. That is the quickest way to form distrust with your clients.

Have you ever received a coupon to your favorite store and tried to redeem it and it did not work? Infuriating! You had an expectation that your coupon would work and be honored. If the company repeatedly makes this mistake, they will begin to be known as not being reputable. Their words were the coupons, but their actions showed them to fall through by not being redeemable. The company's actions of forming mistrust will begin to hold more weight and speak louder than their advertisements.

Finally, on a personal tip, you just can't share your plans and goals with everyone. Not everyone wants you to succeed. Everyone isn't wishing you the best. Some, want to leech off your ideas. I've heard many horror stories of people who shared plans with associates only to have those ideas stolen and executed without them. Unfortunately, it's a cruel world. And, people do not always have the best intentions. So, it is imperative that you are careful about who you allow in your inner circle. You should surround yourself with people who are like-minded and driven. If you do so, more chances than not, you all are working toward something, so no one has time for back-biting or underhanded tricks. You all just want to support each other, make a positive impact, and succeed. So, trust your vibes, lean into your instincts, move in silence, and let your work speak for you. As Denzel Washington said in his portrayal of Frank Lucas in the film *American Gangster*, "The loudest one in the room is the weakest one in the room."

G Code: "When you build in silence, people don't know what to attack." – Anonymous

Do the Unexpected

When you think of the people who have been fortunate enough to have longevity in their careers, they are the people who have been unconventional in their thinking, fearless in their actions and have the remarkable ability to reinvent themselves. You must constantly push the limits of your craft to become legendary and leave a lasting impression. Do not seek to merely follow the trend, that will only provide short-term gains. You should seek to set trends, that will provide long-term success.

The unforgettable ones are the people who thought outside of the box by doing the unexpected and it proved beneficial. Run DMC partners with Aerosmith for "Walk this Way," = iconic. In 1990, Keenan Ivory Wayans created and produced *In Living Color*, a sketch comedy show that was not only funny but provided relevant social commentary and launched the careers of several legendary actors such as Jamie Foxx, several members of the Wayans family, and Jim Carrey = groundbreaking. In 1992, HBO premieres Def Comedy Jam setting a platform to showcase hip hop culture and comedy = legendary. Dr. Dre creates "Beats by Dre" and diversifies his career from rapper/producer into businessman and billionaire status = inspiring. Three 6 Mafia wins an Academy Award for best song for "Hard out Here for a Pimp" from the movie *Hustle & Flow* and sets a new standard for how far rap music can go = outstanding. Then there is Sean Combs, a.k.a. Puff Daddy or Diddy, who after being fired as Vice President of Uptown Records, goes on to start his own label, Bad Boy Records, and makes us all "take that, take that," with countless hits in music, television, film, clothing, and liquor = tenacious.

Diddy has actually always been someone I've admired. His creative energy, drive, and unwillingness to let anything stop him has been inspiring to me. To this day, the way he officially launched the careers of the first two artists on Bad Boy Records in 1993 is a stellar example that I continuously point to of a Marketing campaign that does the unexpected.

If you are in the music industry, then I am sure you know the struggle of trying to push a demo of your music. Radio Program Directors receive countless numbers of submissions that often end up in a trash can or piled up in the corner of a room somewhere. Knowing this, Diddy comes up with an unforgettable way to push his artists' music to the forefront. He introduces the Notorious B.I.G. and Craig Mack by packaging their music to resemble the McDonald's Big Mac sandwich. The cardboard burger box was labeled "B.I.G. Mack," and had a collaborative promotional cassette tape. Side A included music from Craig Mack, with his smash single, "Flava in Ya Ear." Side B featured music from Biggie, including his debut single, "Juicy."

Imagine getting what looks like a McDonald's burger delivered to you? Of course, you're going to listen to what's in that package. And, because Puff Daddy was a student of the game before he was a mogul, he made sure the musical product was ready to be heard. The package was accompanied by an image of the rappers with Puff in an actual fast food restaurant holding the "B.I.G. Mack" and Bad Boy Records branded cups and merchandise. A truly innovative and unexpected image that is priceless, especially now since unfortunately both Biggie and Craig Mack are deceased. If you've never seen this image, you should definitely Google it.

Innovative is not just an industry buzz word. It should be a mindset that you aspire to daily. How are you striving to be new, trailblazing, and influential to your industry? These are checkpoints that you should be referring to often as you continue to learn and grow in your field.

G Code: "My style is to take something unexpected and make it into a hit. That's what I do." – Timbaland

Lagniappe

I hope this book has set you on a path to success for your Marketing and Branding efforts. After reading this book, you should have a solid foundation to build lasting and effective campaigns. I just wanted to leave you with a little lagniappe (or extras) as we say in Louisiana ...

Your career and life should be guided by three main principles: Joy, Patience, and Wisdom.

Marketing and Branding can be brutal at times. It is fast-paced and often filled with long hours. But, if you are passionate about your clients and the work you are producing, then it won't really feel like work. You'll have joy in not only the outcomes but in the process. My dear Uncle, Rev. Louis Griffin, III, used to say that, "You can get tired *IN* it, but you should never get tired *OF* it."

This industry takes patience. There is no such thing as an overnight success. Brands are not built overnight. Consistency over time builds success. Slow and steady wins the race.

Wisdom is not just about the kismet meeting between knowledge and experience. It is about learning from your mistakes, taking sound advice from others, and being willing to share what you've learned. There is no point in gaining a wealth of wisdom to keep it all to yourself. A part of wisdom is acknowledging that you have a duty to share your knowledge with those around you because as I keep saying, we are truly better together.

Extra Saucy Lagniappe

I wanted to end the glow-up edition of this book by giving some extra sauce to make your Marketing and Branding efforts even better! So, I have included some tips on topics that I am often questioned about. I know if you implement these quick and easy steps, you will be pleased with the improvements to your brand.

First up is repurposing and revamping. To repurpose something is to make adjustments that allows it to be adaptable. Repurposing content is one of the best ways to work smarter, not harder! Now, don't get me wrong, people aren't fools. You cannot keep saying the same thing and just change a word or two here and there. Repurposing content is about adjusting how your information is presented, either in a different format (platform), or tailoring the message to appeal to varying audiences of interest.

I often hear new entrepreneurs and small business owners who feel inadequate for not having multiple offerings for their customers. Just because you may only have a few products, or even just one product or service, doesn't mean that you cannot repurpose how you present your content in multiple ways. For example, you can turn blog posts into a podcast, or break up your content into multiple social media posts.

Revamping your content usually requires a little more creativity in how it is presented. Revamping requires updating existing content to include updated statistics or relevant anecdotes. It can be reposted to the same platform, but you'll need to have a hook to get someone to revisit the same content (even though it now includes new information). For example, I once wrote a blog post about what independent artists need to know when attending The Stellar Awards. I later revamped that same post to include information on how to be considered for an award nomination, along with effective networking tips. I was able to direct people to the same place (my website) to see the updated blog post.

Glow-Up Activity

Considering what you've just read about repurposing, use the space below to brainstorm some content ideas. Then, think of how you can repurpose them (for example, a Pinterest board into a blog post, or turn existing content into several infographics).

<u>Original Content Idea</u>　　　　　　**<u>Repurposed Idea</u>**

Use the space below to take an existing social media post and revamp it. For example, you may have a line of novelty t-shirts. Revamp how you present that shirt to appeal to customers looking for Valentine's Day gifts, then for a graduation present, or for a holiday gift.

Glow-Up Activity

I'm sure you know how impactful a kiss can be. A kiss can either seal the deal or stop the train before it even leaves the station. The same is true for a kiss in Marketing. Next up is the kiss. K.I.S.S. = Keep It Simple, Sweetie!

Make it as simple as possible for your audience to find you. It is difficult when your usernames are different for each social media platform. Or worse, if your username has nothing to do with your business or personal brand. For example, your bakery name is "Cupcake Dream" and your username is "@BossyLady." WHAT?! Your username should be the same as your business name (if possible). At the very least, it should be close to your name or at least have the same elements so when a potential customer is searching for you, then the odds are better that you will be found. For example, if your username at least had the word "cupcake" in it, you would be included in filtered results and the chances of you being found is greater.

Use the space below to list your social media usernames. If needed, change them to be the same across all platforms. If the name you desire is not available, try to get the names as close as possible. The same consideration should be taken when deciding on your website URL.

- Facebook:
- Instagram:
- Twitter:
- Snapchat:
- LinkedIn:
- Website URL:

Glow-Up Activity

Despite the insurgence of social media as a means to communicate and connect, the press release is still a relevant and needed tool in Marketing. Press releases can be utilized in two ways; before an event, to make the public aware in order to gain attendees, or after an event, to increase publicity for the promoter or organization. It is important to know which is most important to you in order to send the type of release that is most beneficial to you. In some cases, people will send pre and post event press releases, but keep in mind that news outlets are bombarded with solicitations. So, being precise in when and what you release will serve you better than spamming the media.

Be sure to include the following in your press releases:
- Good contact information (email, phone) – don't make it hard for the media to follow up with you in case they need additional quotes or details.
- An effective date to release details
  - "To Be Released on February 18, 2020" or "For Immediate Release"
- A catchy headline that hints at the "what/why" of your release.
- The body of the release should include all relevant information. Be sure to include not only what you want the media to share, but also how the reader can respond to your call to action.
- Include a news-worthy quote from a relevant participant that is tied to the content of the release.
- Be sure to include a boilerplate, which is an "about us" section at the bottom of the release that gives a brief description of who is sending the document.
- Supplemental photos are always welcome.

Below is an example of a press release I used to advise news outlets of a benefit concert I threw in 2018. Use it as a template to create your own release. Accept it as my gift to you ☺.

Bold Talent. Innovative Results.
Contact: Letrece R. Griffin
Email: Letrece@LetreceG.com
www.LetreceG.com
Phone: 225-288-3184

FOR IMMEDIATE RELEASE
July 12, 2018

Power Move Management Presents: "Back to Church" Benefit Concert for It Takes a Village BR

Baton Rouge, LA: Power Move Management (PMM) will host "Back to Church," a benefit concert on behalf of *It Takes a Village BR*, which is a nonprofit organization approaching its third year of operation. They are dedicated to serving the homeless population with wholesome meals, clothing and hygiene products in the Greater Baton Rouge community.

PMM's Founder, Letrece Griffin, will be celebrating her birthday, and decided to throw the benefit concert to not only bring together friends and community, but to support the charity. "I am inspired by the work that It Takes a Village BR does. Their heart for outreach and consistency in providing meals and support is touching. This concert is a way to bring attention to their organization and garner support," Griffin stated.

The benefit concert will feature Marcy Fisher & Highly Favored, Nancy Armstrong, Arthur J. Gremillion, and Joel Jones & 3MC, along with other surprise musical guests. The concert will be held at Love Alive Church (5522 Jones Creek Road, Baton Rouge, LA) on August 12th at 6 PM. Pre-sale tickets are on sale now for $5 via www.LetreceG.com. Donations can also be made via that website for those unable to attend the concert but still wishing to lend support

Griffin's roots in Gospel music runs deep. She has managed and provided marketing and branding services to national and local Gospel artists. She was featured in Folklife in Louisiana for her expertise and knowledge of Gospel music and tradition. She also spearheaded landmark Gospel events such as The Belle Gospel Concert Series that was held at the Belle of Baton Rouge Casino & Hotel.

The "Back to Church" concert is an extension of her passion for the music that brings her community together and provides so much light and encouragement to listeners.

####

About Us:
Power Move Management & Consulting, LLC (PMM) is a marketing and management boutique agency. Using innovation and new media, PMM assists businesses, organizations and artists with attaining national exposure.

Made in the USA
Columbia, SC
27 January 2023

10478107R00057